Tom's M[illegible] Mop

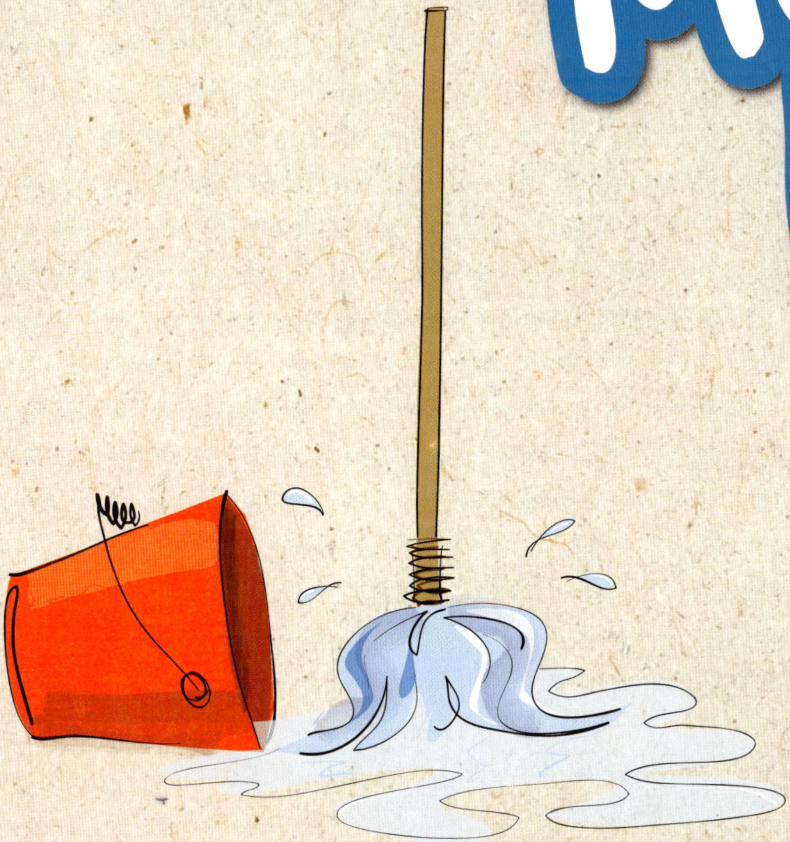

Written by Celia Warren
Illustrated by Bill Ledger

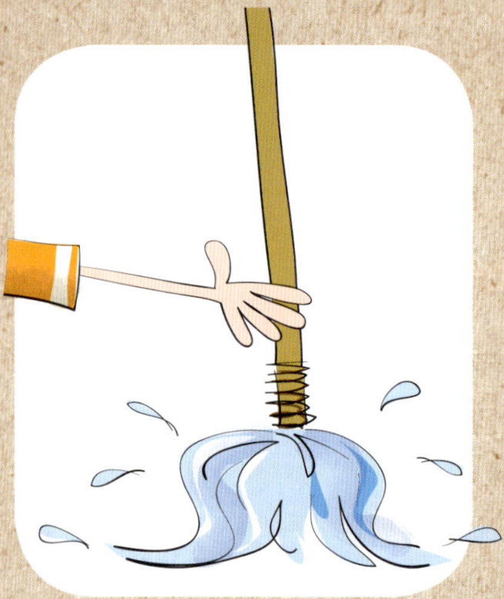

Tom got a mop.

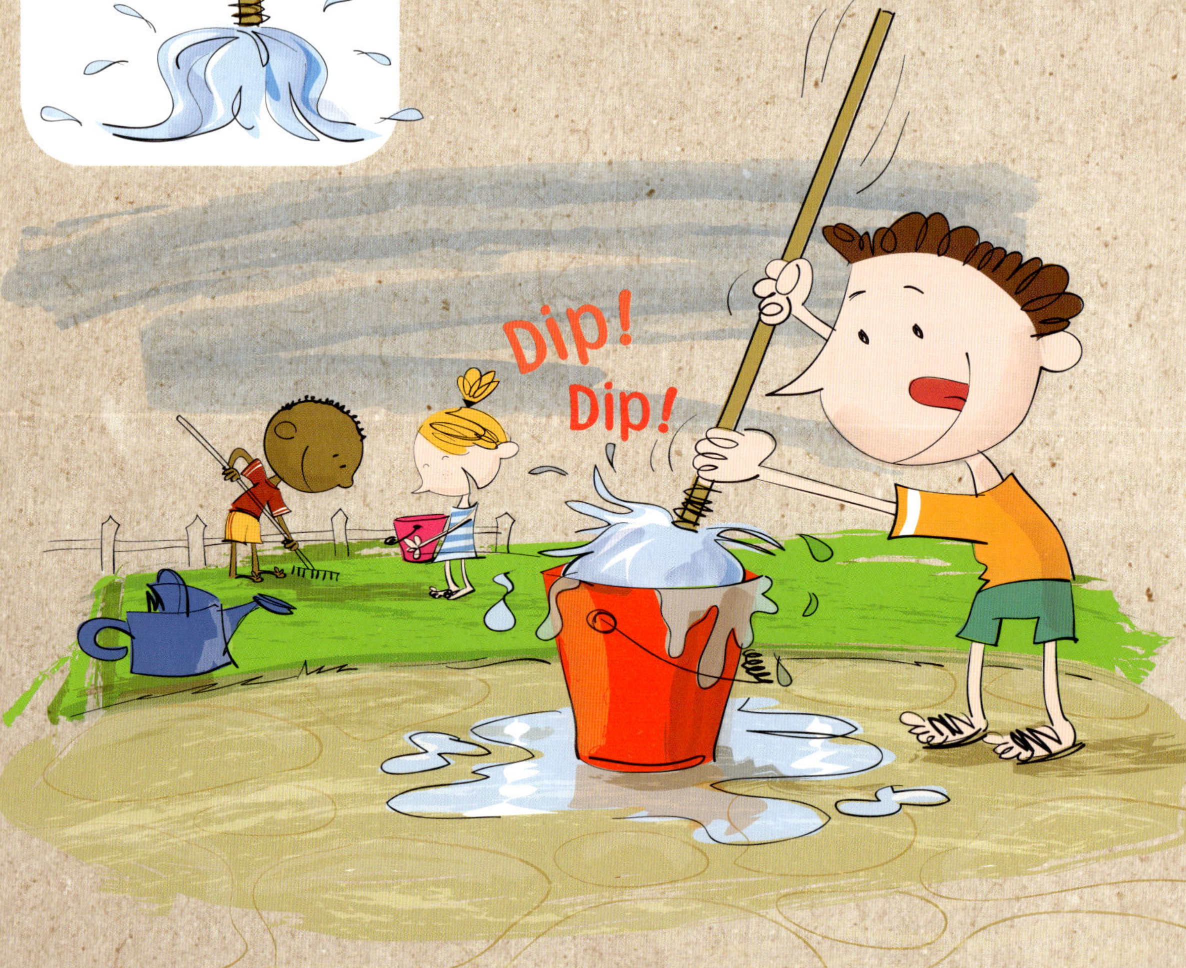

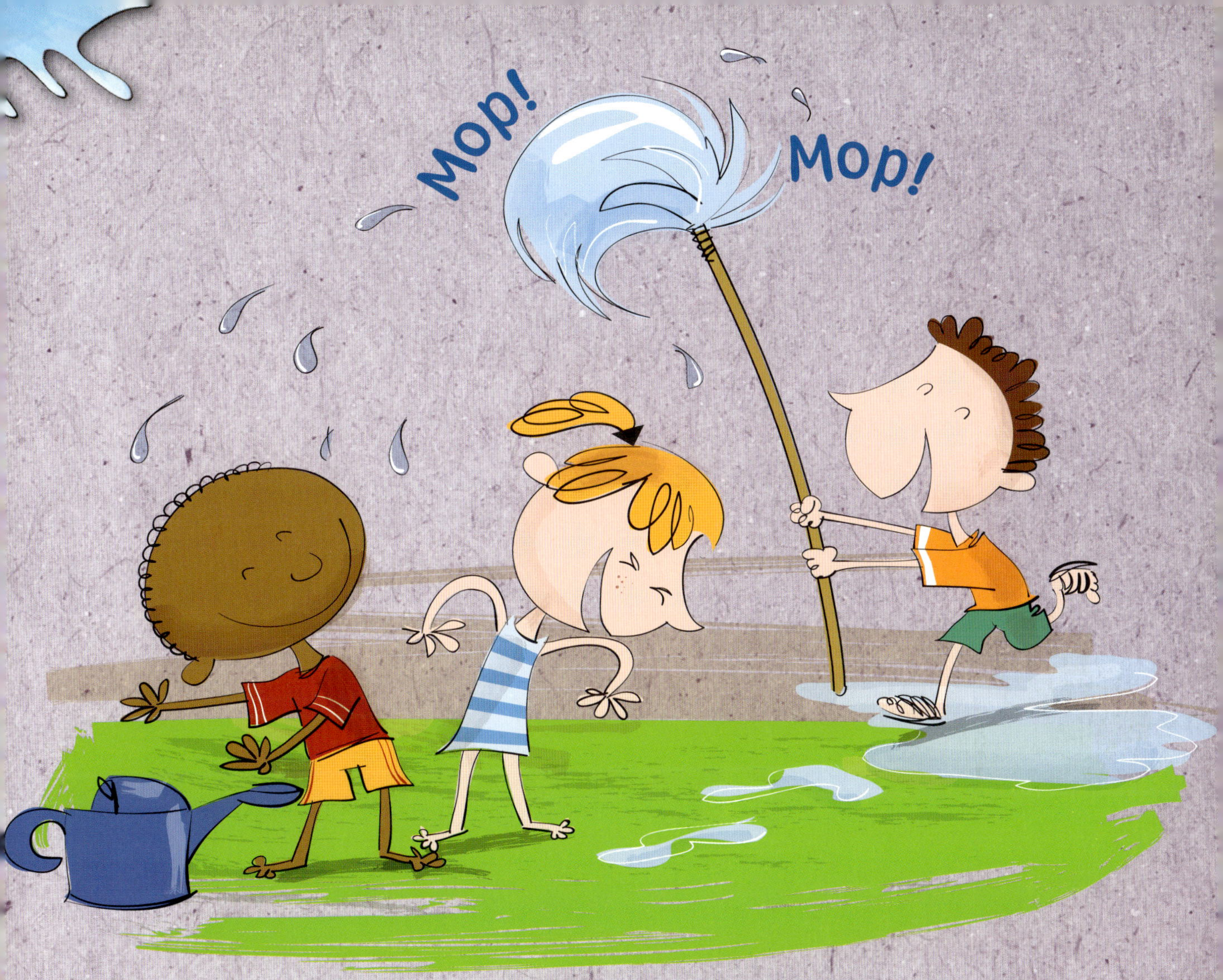

Tom's mad mop got
Kit and Mags.

Kit got Tom's mop.

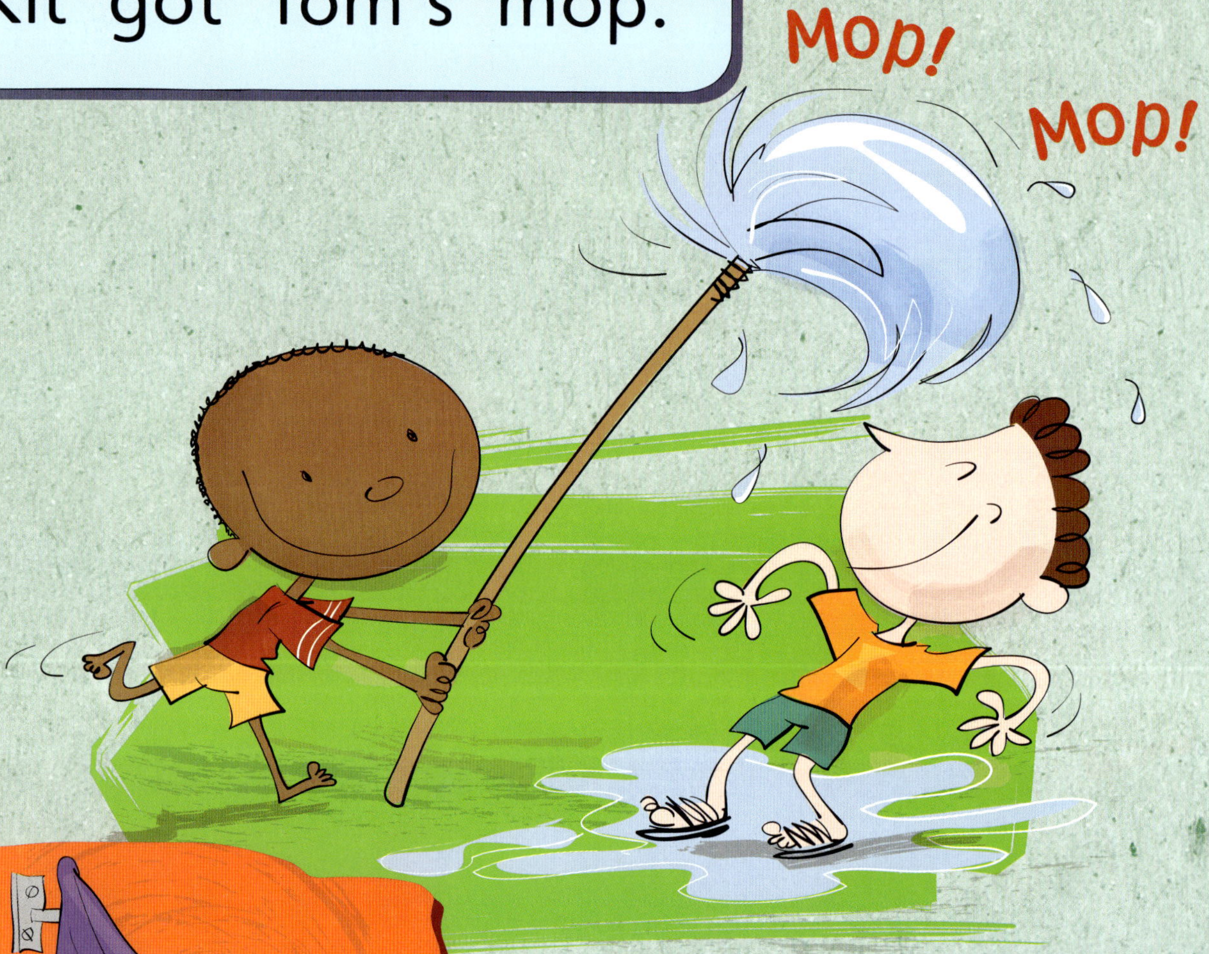

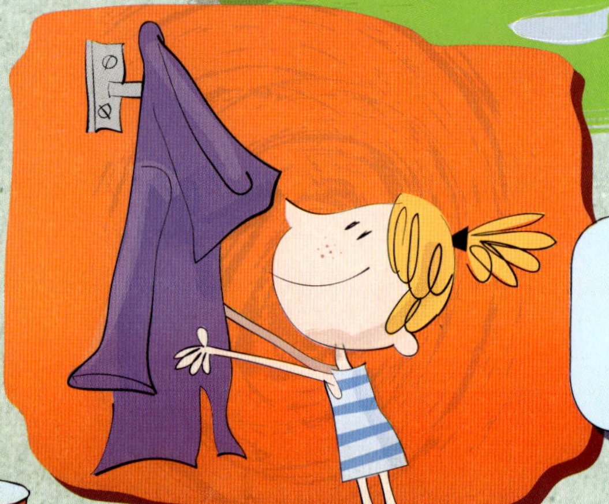

Mags got a mac.

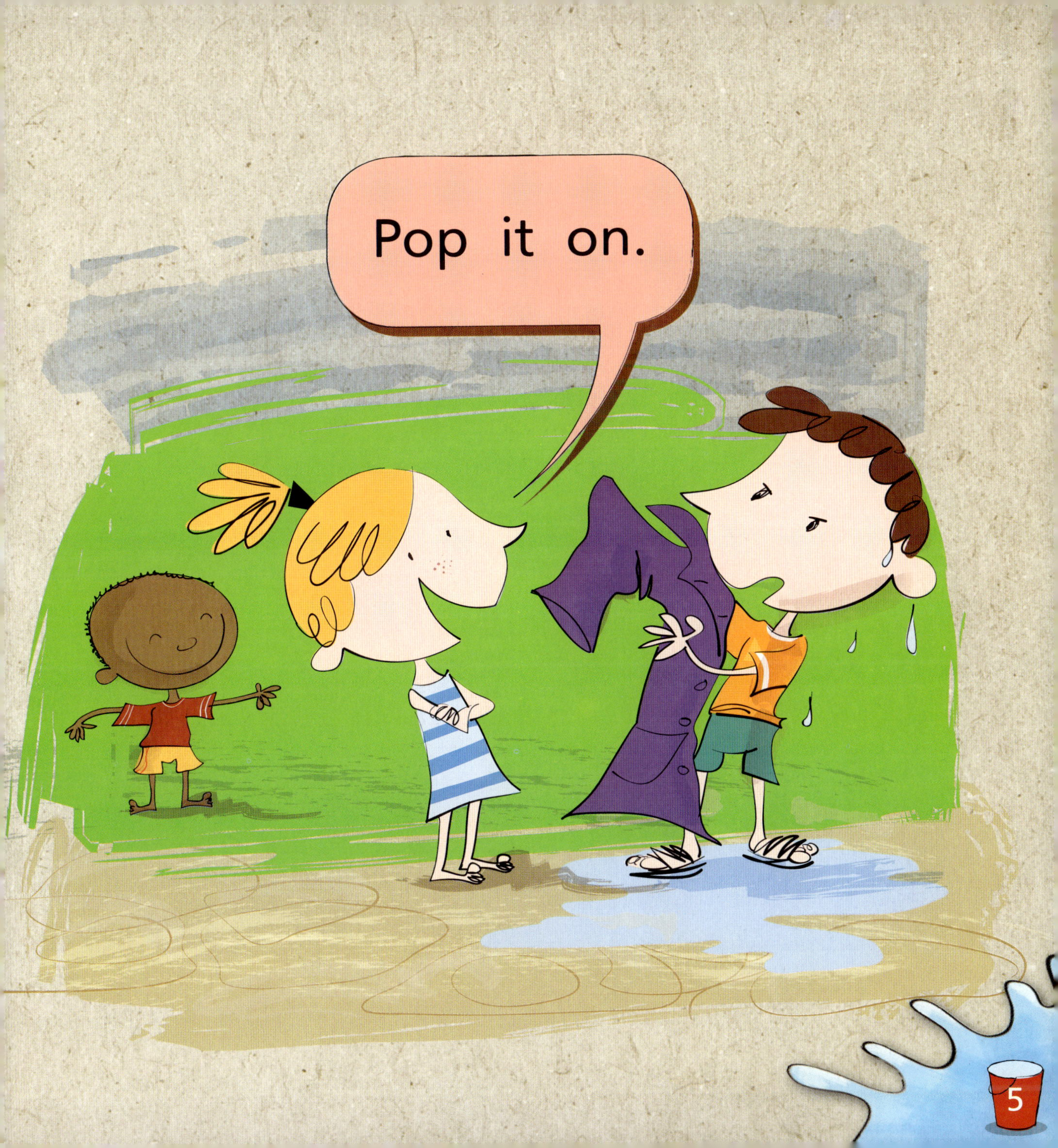
Pop it on.

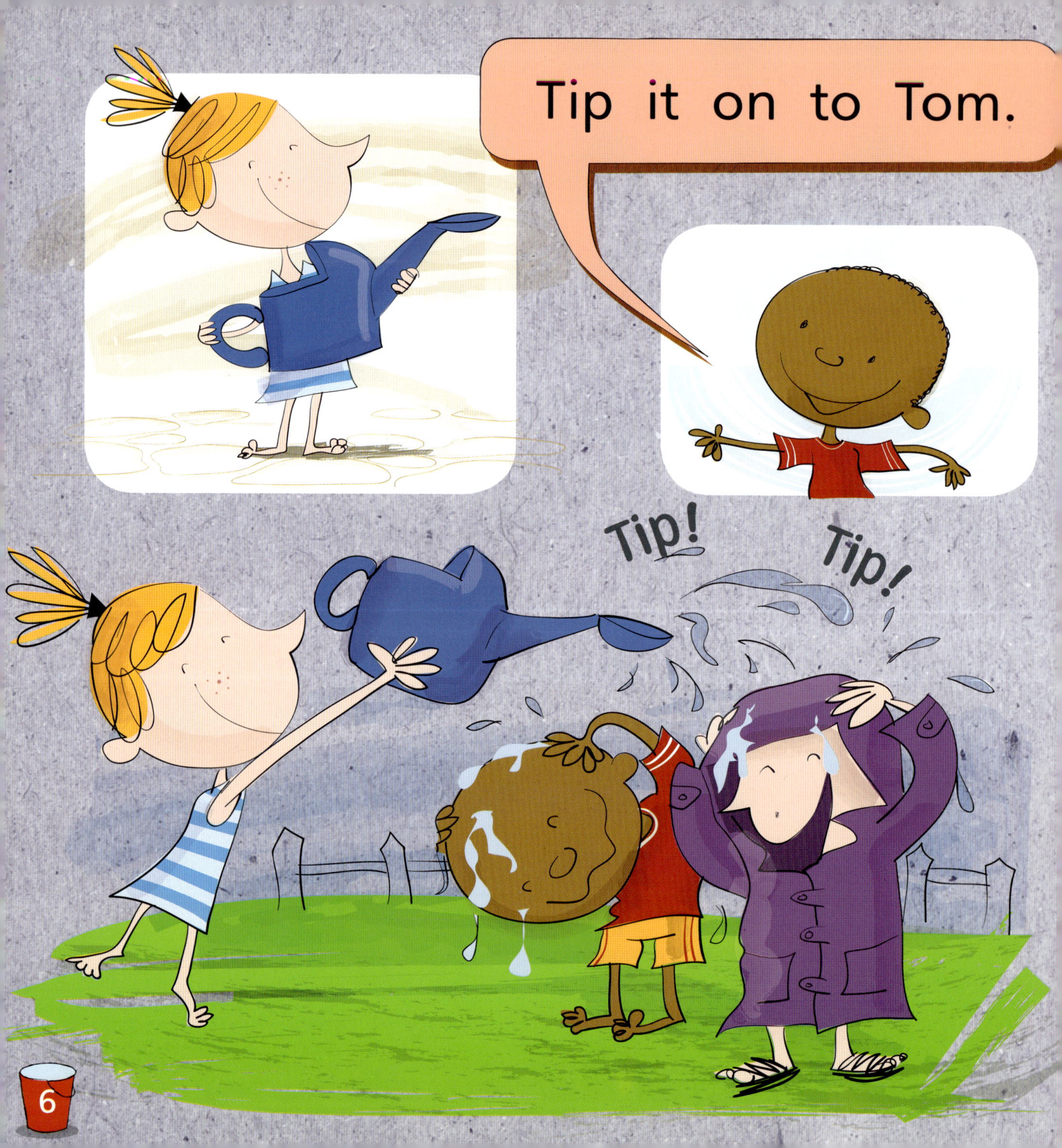
Tip it on to Tom.
Tip!
Tip!

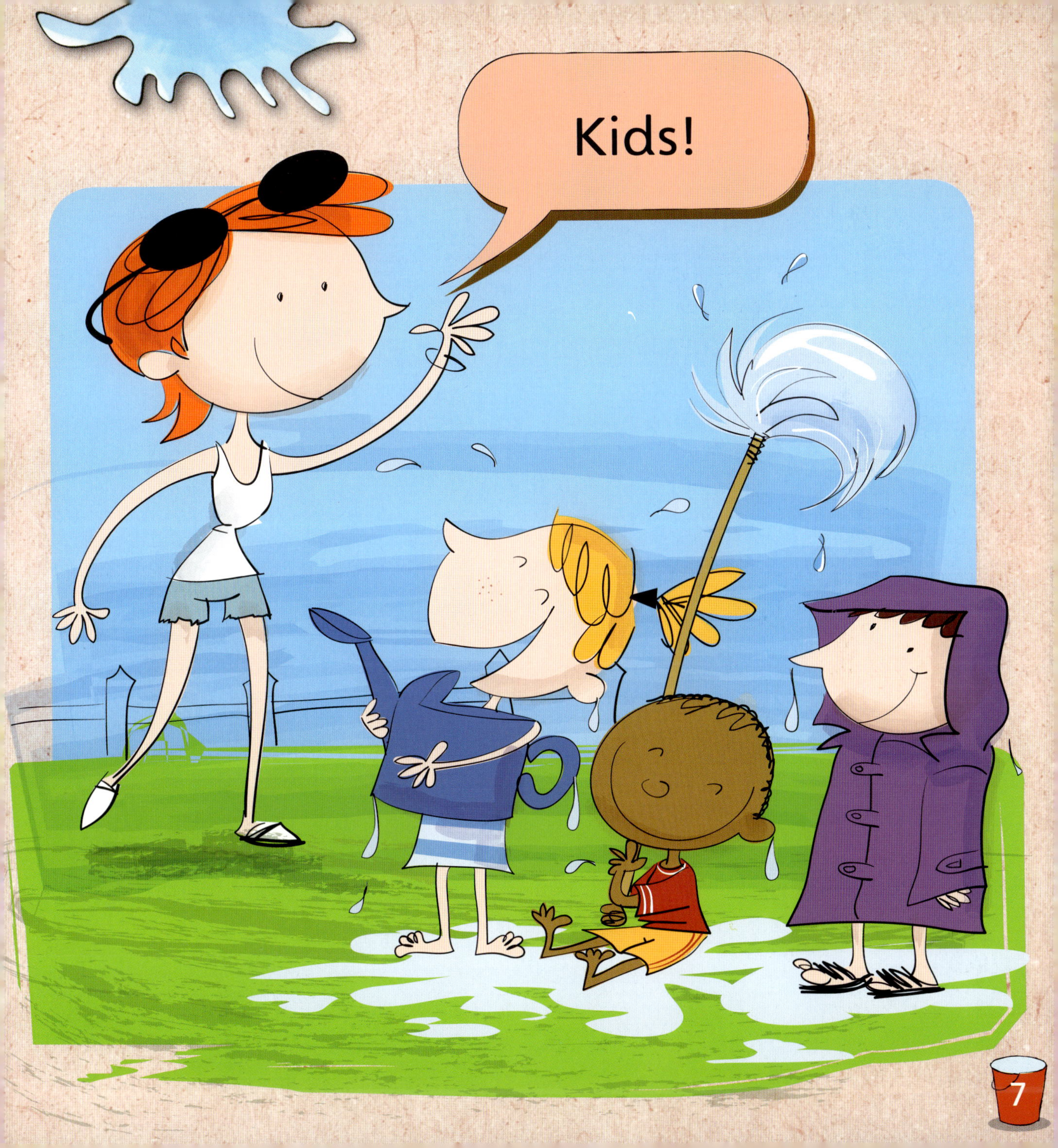
Kids!

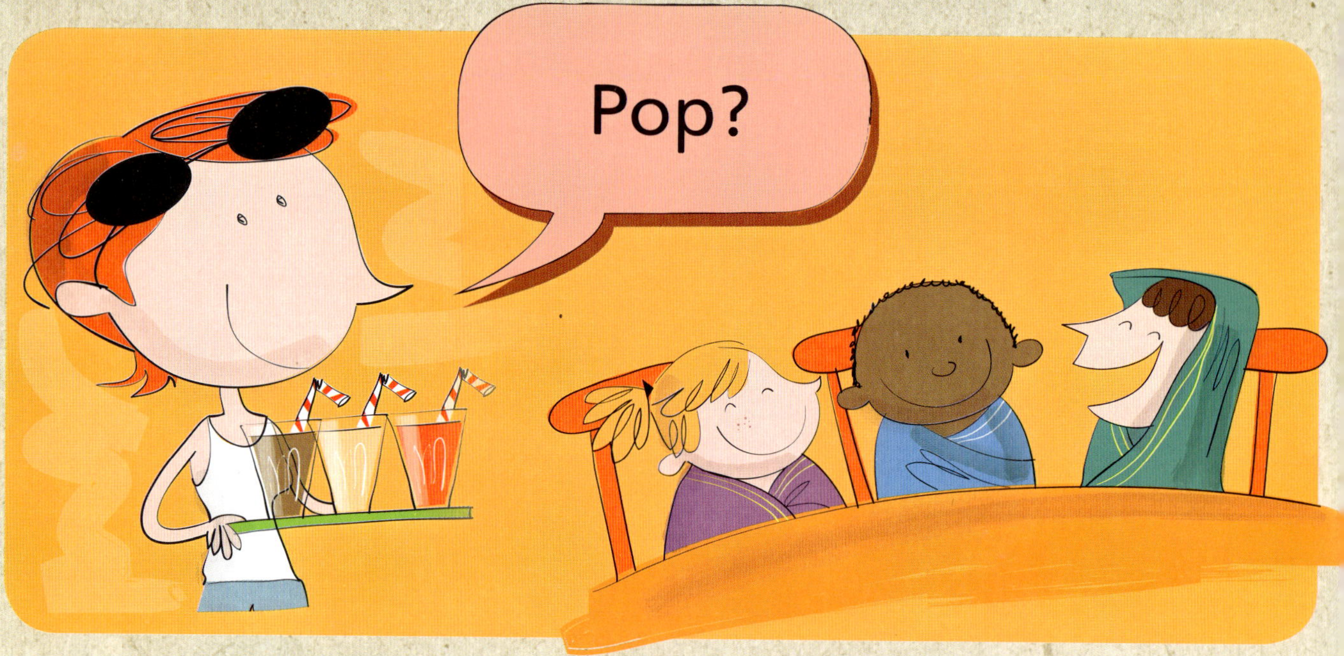

Tom nods.

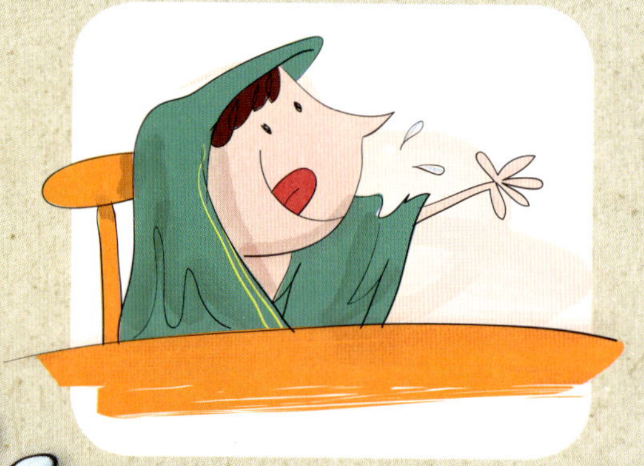

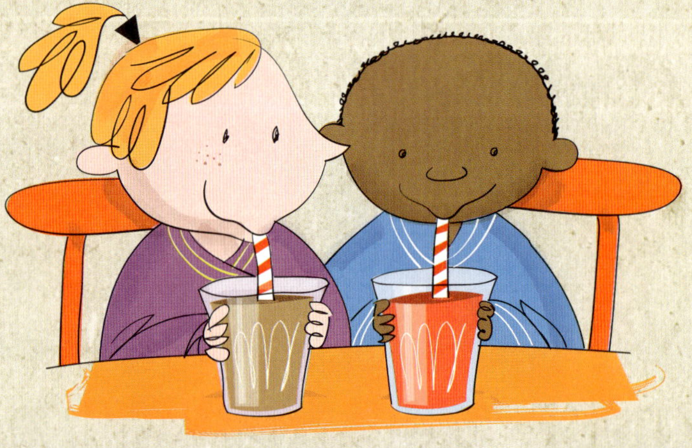

Mags and Kit sip.